I0153256

# SHEARSMAN

## 145 & 146

## WINTER 2025/2026

GUEST EDITOR
**KELVIN CORCORAN**

FOUNDING EDITOR
**TONY FRAZER**

*Shearsman* magazine is published in the United Kingdom by
Shearsman Books Ltd
P.O. Box 4239 | Swindon | SN3 9FL

*Registered office*: 30–31 St James Place, Mangotsfield, Bristol BS16 9JB
*(this address not for correspondence)*

EU AUTHORISED REPRESENTATIVE:
Lightning Source France, 1 Av. Johannes Gutenberg, 78310 Maurepas, France
Email: compliance@lightningsource.fr

ISBN 978-1-84861-999-9
ISSN 0260-8049

## Subscriptions and single copies

Current subscriptions – covering two double-issues, each around 100 pages in length – cost £18 for delivery to UK addresses, £25 for the rest of Europe (including the Republic of Ireland), £28 for Asia & North America, and £32 for Australia, New Zealand and Singapore. Longer subscriptions may be had for a pro-rata higher payment. Prices are likely to rise in 2025. Purchasers in North America and Australia will find that buying single copies from online retailers there will be cheaper than subscribing, especially following the recent drastic price-rises for international mail. This is because copies are printed locally to meet such orders from online retailers. Due to recent changes regarding the treatment of low-value cross-border shipments into the EU, and now the USA, purchasers in there are recommended to use EU-based online retailers.

Back issues from nº 63 onwards (uniform with this issue) cost £9.95 / $17 through retail outlets. Single copies can be ordered for £9.95 direct from the press, post-free within the UK, through the Shearsman Books online store, or from bookshops. Contact us regarding earlier issues (i.e. nos. 1–62), whether for single copies or a complete run.

## Submissions

*Shearsman* operates a submissions-window system, whereby submissions may only be made during the months of March and September, when selections are made for the October and April issues, respectively. Submissions may be sent by mail or email, but email attachments are only accepted in PDF form; submissions may also be made through the upload portal on the Shearsman website (on the *Contact* page). We aim to respond within 3 months of the window's closure, although we do sometimes take a little longer.

## Acknowledgements

We are grateful to the Casanovas & Lynch Literary Agency, Barcelona, acting for the author's Estate, for permission to print the translations of Mercè Rodoreda in this issue. The poems are drawn from the second edition of Mercè Rodoreda, *Agonia de llum*, ed. Abraham Mohino Balet (Godall Edicions, Barcelona). Copyright © Institut d'Estudis Catalans

*This issue has been set in Arno Pro, with titling in Argumentum. The flyleaf is set in Trend Sans.*

# Contents

Lucy Hamilton / 5

Alan Baker / 8

Penelope Shuttle / 11

Biljana Scott / 18

Steven Taylor / 22

Dorothy Lehane / 25

Ian Davidson / 28

Ophira Adar / 31

John Goodby / 35

Peter Robinson / 39

Andrew Taylor / 43

Lynne Hjelmgaard / 47

Colin Campbell Robinson / 50

Ellen Harrold / 54

Aidan Semmens / 56

Adam Flint / 59

John Latta / 63

Peter Larkin / 69

Iain MacLeod / 74

Alexander Gaul / 78


Catullus / 83
*translated from Latin into Polari by Jennifer Ingleheart*

Dmitry Blizniuk / 86
*translated from Russian by Yana Kane*

Vicente Huidobro / 91
*translated from Spanish by Tony Frazer*

César Vallejo / 94
*translated from Spanish by Valentino Gianuzzi*

*Notes on Contributors* / 96

# Lucy Hamilton

## The vigour of animals

I

A worthy Tonto. I was inside the twin pram driving not perambulating. With his red mane flying the horse Silver aka my brother was galloping down the canyon towards the Holt Road. Next thing a robber shot me through my greenstick clavicle and I hurtled out. At that time before a later time I couldn't foresee the fractured sapling that would snap my mother's judgement. At this time I knew the Lone Ranger was also my brother Androcles but couldn't show my pain. Unlike the lion I could speak therefore it was braver not to. My mother thought otherwise when she undressed me and saw the blue ruins. I admired them in the mirror. A worthy Tonto.

II

It all depends on the fulcrum. The Lone Ranger saved his horse Silver from an enraged buffalo. In a reciprocal act Silver chose to renounce his wild life to carry him. If conscience exhorted the Ranger to release Silver back into the wild what prompted Silver to return bringing his friend Scout to transport Tonto. My oldest sister chose to support our dying sister then her dying grandchild. Now with the passage of time she doesn't want to saddle her own children. Is it all about weight this act. Balance as proportion Interdependence. Will her children's children support their mothers. It all depends on the fulcrum.

# Collecting clocks

I

It was all about time. Silver galloped down the canyon hurling me out of the carriage. Then I was in the bath in a plastercast and sling under my mother's tender eye. But in a later time my mother's mind and heart were fragile. When my friend's gentle pony Pudding took fright he shied and careened onto the lawn. I lost my stirrups and glancing up in the nick of time grabbed a branch to swing myself free of the saddle. Then the fractured sapling was under a splint. As I saved my neck the sapling split and my mother's reason slipped. Her life was in *pausis mēn*. Mine *pre puberatum*. It was all about time.

II

The clocks multiplied. I tried to unravel the workings to make them chime at the same time. At dawn I ran to the woods in my brother's shorts and S-belt to sit against a birch amongst woodlice and centipedes. The birds' eyes were wide to the world's instant as they sang to rhythms instinctive to time. My twin exchanged rabbits to breed and sell. If we disturbed the doe's nest she ate her tiny naked babies. The gardener was George Buck. Now Pandemic-distanced under my twin's patio heaters we're toasting our December birthday. Reminiscing to the measure of diminishing red. The clocks multiplied.

# What the faces exposed

I

I was deeply shaken. We were under my twin's bed each digging a thumbnail into the other's tender ear-lobe to see who'd surrender. Suddenly I heard a whimper. It came from a place I didn't recognise. I unscrewed my eyes. I stared at her face taking in the full import of what I was doing. This is what it was to inflict bodily pain on another. I lost sensation of the pain she was causing me. Her face was there before me soft round fragile. I was crushing it into this unspeakable contortion. One of her pigtails was resting on my hand which had become a weapon. I dropped my hand like a gun. I was deeply shaken.

II

It wasn't a fair system. I saw my mother approach me through the glass. Her face as white as the split sapling. She must have perceived my terror as I turned and fled to the woods. I sat trembling against a tree. I became aware of this world I loved. The birds that seemed to trust me when I climbed. The rare oriole I heard in the dawn chorus. My *Observer's Book* said it 'suffered from the man with the gun'. Slowly it dawned that in animal aggression there is no choice or judgement. Only the instinct to survive. Yesterday my twin texted about supporting our beloveds and each other if it should come to that. It wasn't a fair system.

# Alan Baker

## *from* 'A Book of Psalms'

> The small nouns
> Crying faith
> —George Oppen

> "I am like a pelican of the wilderness: I am like an owl of the desert.
> I watch, and am as a sparrow alone upon the house top."
> —Psalm 102

## Psalm 19

The sea-roads were my home, the wild geese my companions
Glaze of frost on the pavement when neighbours shut their doors
My love far from my arms, excess of caffeine wide-awake nights
Sixteen candles there on my wall, here am I the biggest fool of them all
To tread that path since the foundation of the world
Science captures daydreams in its web, give me snowy fields
The watery shore, floes and growlers, bergs and glaciers
From which freedom beckons, shops pull down their shutters
The great original of his generation bedded down in doorways
So I sang, but in my sleep – singing by day is too dangerous

## Psalm 22

Flickerings in REM sleep wake me to insomniac daze
I can't hide from 4 a.m. misgivings, strangled cries
That might be foxes, might be invented, might be
The Last Judgement depicted in a yew tree's branches
Visions revealed under the whitewash of the old church
Or mould on the window sill, spores, canker and gall, infestations
Of mites and thrips, midge larvae and sawfly
Presences once put down to witchcraft, now
To sub-optimal chemical and biological conditions
And soil nutrient imbalance

## Psalm 51

It's the time of moths on balmy evenings
Choosing new wallpaper for the baby's room
Of cloudless blue and the grass like straw
The question drifts like a planet, concerned with
Getting up, commuting to work, meeting a friend for a beer
The dark that had known me all its life, taken by rhythm and decay
Observe the dream lean and tap his shoulder
The winding ways lead to perdition, straighten them
Recursive code leads to a memory leak, patch it
Lost time leads to the present hour, embrace it

## Psalm 53

I want to tell you about the long-horned cattle
Their steamy breath and the ripping sound they make
When they tear at the grass, whose corpuscles are as red
As yours and mine, their neural pathways a labyrinth
Of imagined grasses and steamy byres
Among the scrapyards and small factories
In the cold and empty bus station at midnight
I want to remember the long-horned cattle as I see them now
Through the smudge on the windscreen

## Psalm 61

I'm lost among medicinal cabinets, polished oak and calamine lotion
Searching for a Cortado, a Frappuccino, the quiet hum of dissent
Paradise Reimagined in soft-focus Americana
I frequent charity shops and nail bars, garden centres
With limited offer compost and hardy perennials
Discounted dahlias demonstrate the ruinous state of modern horticulture
The offers more limited, peat left on the moors
To nurture dreams of rewilding and swinging gibbets

## Psalm 62

I stepped and did not step into the same dark
And did not meet the woman I loved after all these years
The path did not take me through woods, night-jar dim and no 5G
No pillow-talk between galaxies, no eavesdropping stars
And my story, friends, starts and ends at a kitchen table
Keep it simple: bread and wine, the surrounding night
And morning will reveal more rooftops, not a single tree
She glides across the evening like a parabola
Like a striking resemblance to your sister
Lost long ago in those very same woods

# Penelope Shuttle

## A Miscellany Presented to Miss Furnival on the Eve of her Departure

May is falconry    September is a long way off
When you are a moth, fear the flame

Earth and air will offer you no baptism to speak of
If you are a girl, fear the night bus

The hand-fed lamb trusts everyone
If you are a child, fear a step-parent in a good mood

January is a loner    April is a plague of skylarks
When you are a rose, fear the rose-bug's tiny chomp

A silhouette is made of stiff black paper and nothing else
Fear north, south, east and west

In Fear's household spices are brought obediently at the whim of the cook
Fear is turreted and tricked out, a castle where no one laughs

If you are the Duke of Clarence, fear your brother the king
gracious though he be

Take the blessing of Saturn    use it when you are shivering in a layby
When you are a jester, fear those who laugh loudest

November speaks cold dialect    March is bindweed, an unwanted suitor
When you are sewing resist the compulsion to work in poor light

February is a wolfskin    June bears the bell
When you become king wear your crown but five times a year

October kneels to the sun    August is the year's ghost
Fear the colour green, for it is the colour of the Fae

If offered a visit to the tombstone factory in Toledo, decline at once
Fear any question accompanied with tongs and pincers of iron, fires

July is a heretic   she has much learning
If you are a girl, fear the owl, fear the owl's child

When you are a lion, fear pentacle and spell-book
If you become a weapon, a Danish axe, for instance, fear rust

Always choose cheerful horses, it is more convenient
Beware the endless knot of the five joys

Learn from the spider who sucks up sweet dew through her web
Fear the man who bears The Virgin on his shoulders

Jupiter and Venus are circling the harbour
Fear the early British Kings and all their prayers

When you dance all night
fear love when it arrives   concealing the truth

then you will be glad of your fear
and take your leave in a quiet manner of your own choosing

almost certainly   by now
the cock will be crowing

## weather in its infancy

to unmarry
to lie low
thinking of the tall sedges
along the Nile,
not yet papyri

*

Spain,
surrounded by snails
Paris,
improved by many small silences

*

it was a poor man's springtime
with a second-hand sun
a hill rolled off a postcard
sent its love xx

*

tongues are motherly
tears are not fatherly
the world is your chapel
may your footsteps always think well of you

*

a collective of mist watchers
a shippen of rain

*

a tree
planting itself

a night train
wandering the streets

*

night and day
I change my name
seeking
the first moment of a tree
oak or ash
but the world
thinks only of herself
longs for ice on the runway

*

an apology scroll:
*I am sorry for etc…*
written in
the most beautiful calligraphic hand

*

a badger's tooth
a frog's nest
a Lenten soup recipe clipped
from *The Tablet*
a prospectus
from The College of Fear

*

time is the snail
nibbling away
at the leaf of the heart

*

clothing the ghost
seen by Emily
in a street dress
of scarlet chiffon

*

days of high summer
but June is your death month

the loveliest weather
is shadowed and bleak

midsummer scythes down
the roses
in memory of you

*

plainchant
spurring past a farthing harp

*

November
with a dusting of summer gold
tangled in her hair

*

Britain,
Apollo's other island,
according to Robert Graves

*

I wrote *sorbet*
I meant *sonnet*

*

a newly sharpened rainbow
above the Madonna
washing her hands
in a silver bowl

*

we get caught in a meteor shower
it rips holes in our raincoats
brilliant light shines through the holes

*

I spit
on a blazing green meteor
fallen from heaven
in order to sanctify it

it fizzes away     over the ridge

*

we stuff ribbons
up our noses
in Dimitri mode

*

she feeds the pigs
in her lucky raincoat

the pigs eye her
like astronomers
gazing up at the night sky

\*

god polishes
his best boots
for the funeral
of the earth

\*


the mirror called Znamya:
it means a banner in Russian

it unfolds from the unmanned spaceship
so that reflected sunlight
shimmers over the Arctic Circle

and sheds diamonds over the skies
as far as Toulouse

\*


in comes
scowling Unhappiness
in her frilly white blouse
and tight black skirt

\*


my network
of weather observers
are hard at work
even though I pay them a mere pittance

# Biljana Scott

## The lollipop man 1

*You see that mosque* says the Kosovar kiosk vendor.
His eyes are toffee-brown.
I know those eyes, I think to myself

as I look to where he's pointing. *Ah but perhaps*
*you prefer to see the church beyond it?*
A liquid warmth with conspiratorial sparks –

where do I know them from?
*Yes,* I smile, *I can see both!*
*Good!* he nods, *that's how it used to be*

*in this country too,* his gaze intent as he pauses
– a brief dimple in time into which a dewdrop rolls –
*before the war. But now people prefer to be blind.*

The droplet settles, its reflection quivering into crescents.
*What a good thing that the two of us still have our sight*
I respond as our eyes lock into their own language.

    I know where I've seen those eyes before
    – the lollipop man, a lifetime ago!
    We'd drive to his small kiosk near Geneva

every Saturday for foreign papers and sweeties! Once,
my father insisted that I ask for my caramel lollipop myself.
I stalled. I knew how to ask but didn't know which was better

English or French, *puis-je avoir* or *est ce que…*
Three languages competed in my head
and grown-ups were always so difficult

*If you don't know how to ask for what you want nicely*
*you won't get it!* I wasn't sure how to ask
nor which one was *nicely.* My father made to leave.

Tears welled, muteness rose like fear. I sought
the lollipop man whose smile-sparked eyes
signed *say it!* My vision blurred. We left.

*Let's hope that those who've lost their sight*
*will find it again!* says the Priština vendor
and having given me directions to the Diplomatic Academy

adds: *You speak their language well for a British girl.*
*Better not to speak it here though!* I notice
he doesn't mention the Serbian we're both using

but opts for *theirs.* Difficult. My gaze quivers
then settles again on his eyes, caramel kind, as he adds:
*Be sure to teach them what they need to learn!*


## The lollipop man 2

Somewhere North of Priština, I stop to stretch my legs. Fresh wreaths
lightly veiled with road-dust propped against a war monument. Young
men mostly. I know nothing about their lives, but one quick glance and
I now know something they never did. Unease glides past, dust-veiled.
A winding ascent and a slug-slow driver in the middle of the road who
speeds up every time I pull out distract me from the strangeness of others
knowing what we never will – our own date of death.

The day of my mother's funeral might well have been my aunt's last when,
in mid oration, walking-stick in one hand, the other on her sister's casket
she extemporises about whether my mother had remained a true Slav or
whether she'd defected to some other side *call it English, British, European*
*or even,* looking at me she adds *Scottish* as she rolls her eyes *whatever you*
*will, just not one of us! No longer one of us!* she loses her balance, claws at

the casket and brings the whole show toppling, or very nearly. Those in the front row settle back down.

Fed up with the old man's game I floor my rental car for one last bid to overtake but as I accelerate, he swings out forcing me to swerve. Verge – sheer ravine – no road – just sky – dust-clouds. All instinct&pulse I turn the car *fucking madman* rear-view check&turn-*fuckit*-turn&check a dozen bursts my breath cursed out at every one *Can't a woman even overtake in this chauvinist country?* I speed back past the monument, Serbian I realise. *Bloody idiot!*

*Trust a stupid Westerner to think of gender!* My aunt shakes her head in disbelief when I make it back late to Belgrade. Why doesn't she own a kettle I wonder.
*You're an even bigger idiot than you realise,* she says. *You have no idea what a perfect opportunity you've just overlooked!* I don't.
*Last year a young Serbian journalist was bumped off that same road. Every one of her bones was broken but not her spirit, oh no! She wrote a book about it and made a mint. Imagine, with your British passport...*

An international bestseller about being harried off a mountain then resurrected from the abyss and purged by the flames of hatred – and all that because of a *numberplate*?
*I'd rather write about the lollipop man,* I say as she pours.
*Ha,* she spits, claws digging into the chairback, *Your father's daughter! Where is your partisan spirit!*

## Granny Counsel

I would wake up to see her hands
turning this way then that above her head
as she lay in the twin bed. *To keep my wrists supple*

she said. *You must be sure to marry somebody
from your own people,* was my granny's advice.
*Preferably,* she'd nod sagely, *from your own street.*

I laughed her off, listing my Geneva neighbours
by their many nationalities to demonstrate
how Balkan tribalism had no place here.

*And another thing,* she whispered, leaning in
to impart her wisdom: *Be sure to see a man
out of uniform before you agree to marry him.*

Her name was Savka
but we called her Baba Saveta
for all her worldly counsel.

Sometimes, as I wake up to a lover
gathering his clothes from the floor,
her supple wrists return a *so-so!*

# Steven Taylor

## Garibaldi

My great grandfather's name

attached to the Republican 5<sup>th</sup> Army Corps
which halted the fascist advance on the banks
of the Segre at Mequineza, on Christmas Day
or thereabouts, the remnants of the battalion

ran out of ammunition and retreated
in good order, aware that most of the troops
who had been facing them across the river
had also been Italian. German fighters

from the Condor Squadron
made famous by Picasso (Guernica)
strafed them as they went beyond the city
(Barcelona) and limped their wounded way

towards the border, slipping
into France, exhausted but defiant. My
great grandfather (a hatter) was quite
insane by now, his brain rotted

by the chemical, mercury, unaware
of what was happening. I can't remember
when he passed but he didn't die
for reasons worth remembering

# Gustatory Cells

I take pride explaining to the general reader

what a philosopher actually intended. Jacques
Lacan is one example, reducing him to the size
and suckle of a caramel lozenge, wrapped in
seasonal purple, to be discovered accidently

inside a tin of Christmas toffees. Most people
select a solid chocolate or the softer-centred
sweets that taste of berries, but caramel lasts

which is exactly what he would have wanted

M. Lacan. This is all you need to know


He was born in Paris,
with sophisticated receptors

Language is the house of being

You are slave and I am master
Reverse this order at your leisure

# Homage to Bernini (Louise Bourgeois)

After killing the German officer with a single shot from his rifle

the British sniper returned, pleased as punch, to his unit, whistling

a song that wouldn't be released until the 1960s. It was inexplicable
how he knew the melody. Ode to Billie Joe, recorded as the B-Side
in Los Angeles by Bobbie Gentry for Capitol Records. An amazing
song that appeared to come out of nowhere. Hypnotic, mournful.

Just an acoustic guitar (picked by Bobbie) and added strings.

Four violins and a pair of cellos. The story set in Mississippi.

Whatever they threw off the Tallahatchie Bridge (there was some
debate, but most of us assumed it was their baby) stayed with you
lingered, once you'd heard it. Like nothing else on the radio.

I remember listening, the week I read the comic strip

with the sniper whistling, untroubled by his actions, returning
to his unit somewhere in the Apennines. They were used to
him disappearing. Accepted he was different. Welcome back,

old chap. I think it was in the Victor.

Billy Joe McAllister, sometime later, committed suicide.

# Dorothy Lehane

## Cave Lore

1.

*A mouth coming undone starts at the lips,* wrote Jacques Roubaud.
The cave & love also, coming undone, start[s] at the lips.
It is true that the tongue is an early warning system of both taste
& character. We have too much time & too much mouth.
I'm always leaving, as most songs suggest. What if I surrender to
the trouble? Mythologizing the self is a warning, & a neurotic
pattern. Mythologizing the cave is to lock onto a discourse.
There is locking onto a discourse & then there is the shakedown
of subjects, floating in & out, adding to the project.

*

I admire the project, though I suspect it is doomed. How to
integrate the explorer into the art. The poetic dimensions clash
against the self-referential practice which simultaneously installs
& rejects, operating as a subversion of the standard exploratory
discourse. Who was I to think I could make an authorial
comment or elucidate on caves & their ongoing performance?
My observance versus their perpetual existence through time.
My capacity to comment or add knowledge. Where I am
struggling to exist, caves are simply existing, ancient & for the
most part, unchanged, enacting an ongoing, unscripted
performance, utterly unbothered by my observations.

*

People you lose, want to be lost & people who are lost, do not
want to be found. In the ambit of the complex, each trace of
disturbance is written as a sociality of thought. In German,
*there is a bird in your head* is another way of saying you are mad.
If the lyric essay can teach us anything, it is that it all goes in,

the anti-narrative which over time chimes thematically so
there seems to be a type of narrative functioning, which is a
vulnerable type of moral behaviour. In illness, the lyric essay is
an undoing of filtered consciousness. In poker, you can move
between burning the cards & going all in.

2.

He says I play him like a fiddle, but the assumption
here is that I remember the tune & with that I might
act dishonestly. To be expert in the art of
manipulation. Or the intentions behind actions.
Outpouring to the assembly. To take shelter. From the
Middle English 'sheltron' or 'sheldtrume' or the Old
English 'sċildtruma' or 'sċyldtruma'. These beautiful
layers of meaning: a phalanx or company, a tortoise
formation. The cave is communal, & I'll lay it out for
you. The fiddle must be kept in good working order,
which is not entirely how it feels to play. Today we give
reverence to genuflect, from the Latin root 'flectere' to
bend or even to reflect light, while 'deflect' means to turn aside.

*

If blond girls are what you need, I am blond girls.
Loucheness is the currency. Either loucheness or slaughter.
Are you a systemiser or an empathiser? Robust curiosity
deserves to be taken seriously. Love can step out & sure,
another love will rush in. God, this is ruddy. Really very
ruddy. *Oh god, renaissance woman, what are you doing?*

*

How frequently men monitor our facial responses. *How odd
to have a face,* I said & If I'm honest I was wanting a riposte;
some Levinas, a sort of 'how vulnerable' connection—the
big reveal versus the big conceal. Add stage directions now.
Hit me with a footnote on absence, love, ontology minus the

text itself. Who can read it? Who has permission? Who is forced into the vision that implicates the face. The chorus is a little genealogy, a girl bond, a dancing mania. State the problem: facial gestation or the cave.

3.

Don't close the door on poetry. It is another way of knowing. Where, if I write this for a broader readership, do I place the intellectual reader? How do I structure pleasure? It starts with a body leaving home. The debris of the present against the insistence of something old. That feeling of closed for the winter. Radon, like love, will poison you. Is it love or caves that will help you discover your most enlightened self? That will help manage the inner child who has forgotten how to play?

*

Honestly—how do we enter the poem, if we are this careless with language. If we cohabit. If fluency flies out of the window. If we forensically trace the drift. Jolted by memory, association, mouthpiece. Passively acquiesce under our maladies. There is disease & then there are remarks about disease. For the sake of shaping the landscapes, autoethnography is a pushback. It violates classification. The beautiful way the poet collapses into philosophy. The lamenting of a changing world, disintegrating with doubt, hidden in the poem, perceptible in the headlines. A counterpoint are these controlled cave spaces, which remain full of possibility, unchanged, not moving at full-throttle, not so in-flux.

*

& maybe I do want the audience to be passive, deferential, after all. I am temporally tied, returning to the contoured lines because only they stay the same, because they are out of my realm of knowledge, a haphazard inquiry. Predictable & restful in the face of a world that favours [& values] productivity & systems of knowledge.

# Ian Davidson

## from And why not?

### Feb 26 2024

1.
Dogs bark from both sides

*Things on their minds*

Words on a distant thread

2.
Another course floats by
transparent as jellyfish,
 tendrils in a fluid medium.
The manhole needs more bricks.
I extract them like teeth -
laugh at the gaps.

3.
It do be how it is done.

\*\*\*\*\*\*\*\*\*\*\*\*\*\*\*\*\*\*\*\*\*\*

*Cross Mayo by bus into an uncharted future. Waiting for hours, on corners and crossroads in the warm rain, striking up a conversation as a match flaring, conversation becoming conflagration, lighting up the dark skies.*

Can I imagine my first journey out?
When I have traction I'm happy.
Little engines chug,
Tyres grip.
Don't panic.
The thread takes words from my mouth,
the pen to write them down becomes frayed,
my eyelids grow heavy, drained.

## Feb 27 2024

Living a dog's life every
detail would give pause for thought,
like a detail of soldiers passing the window in 1972.
A dog knows few words; beach, ball, cat.
Fetch is a test,
or come by or sit or leave.
Simple tests
easily completed.

Sitting among friends
I put my head to one side as if listening.
When a ball is thrown I lose my head.


## Feb 28 2024

She coughed between stations
before barking into a phone, cajoling.
No-one else spoke.

Do people always know who is sleeping with who?
That bitch she said.
It is a gateway drug
looking into someone's eyes and lying.

*A ruin has a space into which you can insert yourself. I heave on the stone wall.
One man holds another man around the chest. They heave together. Masonry
is extracted from the ruin. I sit in the space and read.*

## March 1st 2024

St David's day without a daffodil to my name.

*I could have been anyone in that gap left when the block was extracted by two men working together. Working class people work hard. It is in the name stupid. I get off the bus before the end of the route, stare at the sky and the gaps between the stars, looking for someone or something.*

*A spark on a dark night, flaring, or the sluggishness of greying skin stirred into life. The future looks rosy, blushing, spectacles forming then falling away, and then the phone stops ringing.*

I can only imagine life on my own
in the uninhabited spaces

*I wish things would happen sequentially. Eating disorders for example, train rides, getting on and off a story line.*

Books stitched up.
A pen, lying still, no *pen* at all                [Cym: head
but a *cynffon* barely twitching,                [Cym: tail
a tail of a tale.
Losing the plot
like a corpse in an open casket
lying in line
and embalmed
waiting for a resolution.

# Ophira Adar

## Notes on a Life
*After Alisha Dietzman*

A boy knocked out my milk tooth when I was six.
I never let him see me cry.
I have felt the word *love* by mistake.
Some things I liked about you more than others:
your morning breath tasted of nonchalance,
parts of your past that surprised me –
your mother taught you to buy powdered milk,
you grew up in a place where wild horses
became silk under palm.
I have embraced all forms of beauty.
I have rejected all forms of beauty.
My prayers are soft and open slowly,
but act as a dead weight
I do not have strength to carry.
My favourite ice cream flavour is dissent.
I have identified with martyrs, sometimes.
I have seen blue I wanted to swallow whole.
I have often felt angry.
My favourite version of myself is in future tense.
Once I left my home at a late hour
to meet a man whose image stayed with me.
We became taller versions of ourselves,
wisps of smoke above flame. Sometimes
before orgasm, I whisper his name.

*Note:*
This poem is a response to two poems by Alisha Dietzman from her collection *Sweet Movie* (Beacon Press, 2023): Love Poem by Yellow Light' and 'Love Poem by the Light of the Desert'.

# A Calculation of Absences

I have been a woman, once.
Like darkness, my power derived
from the absence of something

changing its meaning in the years
of my life: absence of freedom,
absence of children, absence of God.

The white noise
after the needle lifted its mouth
from the spinning song,

the awareness of a flame
extinguished, finger and thumb
wet with spit, warmed by a quiet heat.

*


I have been a woman, once
in an empty room, the wick cool
and black, the flame running
round the edge of the brass cup.

I could separate heat from flame,
conjure the image of happiness,
change the course of a person's life
once they'd belly-laughed at one of my jokes
or watched me sleep till a late hour
on a modern winter morning.

*


I have been a woman, once
defining myself by minutes and hours;
things I had no control over,
to be measured out neatly
like the cooking of an egg.

I rejected what no longer served me:
romance, sadness, alcohol,
the Gregorian calendar.

I have been mostly interested in the past.
Is this a symptom of sadness?
Concealing oneself.

*


I have been a woman, once
on an aeroplane, leaning back
in the plastic seat, black unravelling
through the window and the turbulence
telling me I might die soon.
It was a comfort to know my last *Shema*
would echo the final words
of millions of others, also unsure
on the topics of afterlife, resurrection,
the question of prophets –
if they can visit us in dreams.

If the antonym of concealing
is to reveal, how can I do it
easily and without shame?

*


I have been a woman, once
looking down at my own body,
my breasts larger
and more motherly than ever,
not milk-filled or freshly kissed,
a reminder of something
I didn't have and no longer knew
I wanted. I was on a journey
towards *non-desire*

the same as desire
but without expectation.

\*

I have been a woman, once
after I became human

in the white heat
of a great city, shaped by things
that had almost happened,
ready to kick off my shoes
and run.

# John Goodby

## 1982: The New Yorkshire School

Workshops seemed to gush like water from the strike -
fluent and peat-stained, but not so's it would hurt you;
*The colour of Tetleys*, said the NUPE man, *and you
drink that*. At which, Beth sliced an onion into her bath
as she ran it, giggling *Gravy, gravy!* She was an artist,
given to such comments, about to paint 'Mr Larkin
Was Very Strict In His Library' to prove it. After Steel
that was, when we drank the Humber ferry dry *en route*
to Scunthorpe (not as *students*, friend, but revolutionaries
working in the student field). There to listen on CB
radio to M18 pursuit tales; of the blue-and-yellow
helical cables of artics from unregistered kipper-ports
secateured in lorry parks outside a Happy Eater. Bliss
was it to be young among tea urns, butties, picket-rotas,
and the power to say what moved and didn't. So that year
became the year of 'That Was The Year When' poems,
of cheques that read *Pay Bearer One Pound Only*, cashed
in the Co-Op Bank, each a pure lyric *Because*, because
come Saturday next the planks had already been laid
across the pool in the Leisure Centre - and, the way
Arthur Scargill would that sunny afternoon, everyone
walked on water. *Ça ira!*, despite the rumours that some
harboured dreams of diving in at the deep end
of moderation, dreaming Sir Bill Sirs. Or, deeper
still, that plans existed in which They might express regret
that *a state of war now exists between this country
and Liverpool*, moving at the pace of Armitage
Shanks's Pony. In that moment, the outraged poet
glaring at the boy in a biker jacket, in a toothpaste-
stripe T-shirt, who wolfs a forbidden sandwich, simply
shows his ignorance of impending heaven. The blows
fell lightly then; a few drops, hardly rain, acknowledged
only to be shrugged off. Meanwhile, caught in the folds

of purple hills, pushing the pillars of a different temple,
a mild Cleckhuddersfax surreal unfurled itself – airs
on a post-YOPs breeze of Small Business Grants, savour
of alphabet soup kitchens, of new vistas ladled out
by rapparees grinning over their roll-ups, coming up roses.


## *from* Six Poems towards a Theory of Friendship as Translation)

*for Tom Cheesman*

Pure experience is the ... immediate flux of life ... Only new-born babes, or
men (sic) in semi-coma from sleep, drugs, illnesses, or blows, may be assumed to
have an experience pure in the literal sense of a *that* which is not yet any definite
*what*...
—William James, *Essays in Radical Empiricism*


We *joie* in what's to do with *Sprache* Tom but so often
miss what language does back          breaks its parole
singing of our limits     staring at the *limen* to be literal
about it or littoral       the thin line of foam the waves urge again
and yet again up the beach sand shells pebbles wrack
glisten in sunlight & view of the far    the offering
The limits of my word are the remits of my wold
in this part of the world to stretch it   Can an event
even happen if not in language is no joke     moot
as the point at which a metaphor becomes dead
that metaphor          being itself a dead metaphor
to discern language signing off       our bounds for once
or to ask when a tree falls in a forest & no-one is there
to hear it       does it really fall       that old chestnut

# A Roman Candle

After three-four murderous blue-stinking circuits
the brakeless grass-track Beezer fizzed you out
of her garden, out through Ada's front gate, gone
to bale out over Lüneburg, not King's Heath,
a card-carrying Red: *Utrinque paratus*. Where,
according to The Great Gardener, Deutschland
should have been put to the plough after the sword –
and you felt he had a point. Yet was made unwhole
again, like you in Lucas's toolshop, while Pollit
or Gallagher hymned the Sino-Soviet split.

Down Keynes' high summers the Plan was pitched,
its tramp of dams, tractors, beets, boots, displaced
in unroped, sheer ascents of Tryfan. Yampy
Tankie, daft and sane to scorn the foreman's job
they dangled! Hungary, the Prague Spring - always
you rise, as from our lawn, glib falling, swept back
always from the Woodbine glued to a thin grin,
Bluebottle to your best buddy's Eccles: *I give
thee sixpence? I will see thee damn'd first!*
Star-gazing twins, to weave a spidered heaven

of red giants' ancient lights, in a coal-shed
the mirror would tarnish that harvested their shine.
*Frank's Book of the Telescope* opens one last time
as if to swallow the glow of *Aurora*-blushing dawns
on the Scheldt, where Bedfords jounced you through *dorp*
after *dorp*, each house surrendering its quilt
from unshuttered upper windows. You tender
a blunt chivalry as redress, the sun's shilling
spinning through your glass-heeled tankard's glow
sinks. Left out, its pewter will cloud in long grass,

dew-roughened, under two apple-trees named
for nephews. (A drunk wasp slips from its rim,
fails to learn butterfly in flat Woodpecker; drowns.)

From the big scarlet box set of *Learning Russian*
cartooned with onion domes, a polar bear, Trans-
Siberian railway, the crumbly, dark-brown voice
of George Osmolensky issues like rye bread: *DA!*
Tonight you fry onions, a sliced sheep's heart.
The steamed-up window is streaming Ursa Major
you will land from, on the sudden morning step.

*Roman candle* = a parachutist whose chute fails to open; *Beezer* = slang for a
BSA motorbike; *Utrinque paratus* = *Ready for anything* (motto of the Parachute
Regiment); *yampy* = crazy; *Aurora* = Russian battleship which fired a salvo to
signal the Bolshevik assault on the Winter Palace in October 1917.

# Peter Robinson

## Italians in Paris

*for Anna Saroldi*

        ...like de Chirico
dreaming of his Turin statues
between sharp-shadowed portico
and farther factory chimney –
or man who stole the *Mona Lisa,*
who suffered from lead poisoning
and hated their *sale macaroni,*
*sale macaroni* raining on the memory
of his neighbour from Luino,
*sale macaroni de mon amour?*

However could he have imagined
Apollinaire might be arrested?
And, Anna, you have got to wonder
how that sorry, tie-less poet
(poet in handcuffs with his lawyer)
could ever have purloined *La Gioconda?*

However could he have imagined
those days spent in La Santé
would spell the end of his affair?
And, Anna, what if *sale macaroni,*
*sale macaroni* raining on the memory
like a shock of chestnut hair
recovered from that other autumn
or his bandaged head like mine,
what if the theft, pandemic, war
(*à bas Guillaume, à bas Guillaume*)
had made *La Gioconda* famous
adding to the cracked allure
her smile would have, come home?

# At the Line End

'"Where is Via de Chirico?"

...

"I don't know.'"


With its lit sign coming towards us
now, no reason not to go,
we would take the number 8 bus
as far as Via de Chirico
to find there's nothing metaphysical
about its dream of springtime
where kids are playing basketball;

no, nothing metaphysical at all
about its cul-de-sac cross street
except perhaps for cloud forms
broody above these suburbs
and their new developments
giving out in farms' fields
of cabbage, sunflower, tomato...

The park named for Juan Miró
sports t-shirt hues right off his palette;
then there's a pond, a bug hotel,
scents of mown grass for the compost,
two pensioners' tentative feet
and mothers with their offspring
running in or out from shadow

on through its dream of springtime
with nothing metaphysical
about this cul-de-sac cross street;
but here we are, I promise you,
under trees' delicious shade
to try and see greens at their best,
see them as if it were our last

40

in Via de Chirico's next to nowhere;
yet still it has its turning circle
where another number 8 bus
(doors open, driver on his phone)
is waiting and will take us – us,
no reason left to go or stay –
back the way we came, as now you know.


## Some Words

> 'Dico alcune parole
> nello spazio vuoto preciso.'
> —Franco Fortini

Dusk-warmed brick façades
in the town's main square,
il Campo, we catch sight of where
the Sala della Pace is
closed for repair

so I don't get to see
Lorenzetti's *Allegory
of Good and Bad Government.*
Still, we sit and stare
at its precise, empty space

never meant to be
the track for a horse race
(I hear a tour guide say)
and echoing in my ear
are their words, words, words

struggling to outface
the latest from our *Bad*
now café table lamps come on
and, love, I need your arm
to help me through the streets

towards that hotel, home,
as their words, words disappear,
for still the enigma smiles
from this precise, empty space
where none of them can save us from all harm.


## The Resort

> 'an overdose of shadows'
> —Rosemary Tonks


Between each wave form and its foam
living daylights will assume
a meaning of their own while you,
back against the seawall's
stonework sadly know what's going on.

High tide is catching up with girls
scampering from the spume
that wraps itself around their ankles
(ankles wreathed with strands of seaweed!)
in this English south-coast town.

Their shrieking mingles with the seagulls
aligned along shut bathing huts
now all occasions do inform
against you, for your God and time,
they've both lost patience with this world.

The landscape's filled with signs and omens
like red sky, rainbow, nervous breakdown
in bedrooms, love, no ifs, no buts,
above the booming breakers
of your fog-bound café…

Then, poet, better not believe them,
whatever the seagulls have to say!

# Andrew Taylor

## Walk in the Lanes
## about St. Domingo

Return
   there's the pull of mapping
& the blackbird at dusk
in competition
with the layers of blue
from the oatmeal horizon

Advance
   the spring tide
it's in the air & in the light
await the silence of Sunday
lane wandering

## July to August

The scent of cut grass & heat
      shade brings relief as does
tepid water from the flask it's
easy to think of the settlers
heading west

light from open shutters
reflected through dusty glass
      a yellow hue like crossing
a bridge at midnight

though the calendar rolls on
Autumn is on show yellowing
leaves fall early

*


at first light losing sight of the hour
keeping tabs using the angle

of the rise over the trees the
    direction that the sheep

move in & the Rome flights'
vapour trails

at the empty breakfast table
cool morning air moving through
the Iberian calls focus on memory
      of early mornings

there goes the sound of sheep
      joining in as the slant shifts
the volume rises a reminder of
location a signifier that beyond

it all ticks by effortlessly if only
the lane still smelt of wild Thyme
        those evening excursions to follow
the sun Andrew drove through

the end of a rainbow & everything
was golden

is light a feeling? The best sunscreen
is a house especially those that play
jazz in darkened rooms at 3.00 p.m.

For Roger the late robin is a gift
the chalkboard list remains
as do her initials with a hastily drawn
heart

crunch of footsteps on gravel
        later than expected
Kenny's leaving for the coast
the sun highlights the wine crate's
lettering

Château Bellefont-Belcier
        Grand Cru Classé
Saint-Emilion Grand Cru

the bands in the wood grain
        are just like the horizon

## 19.29 21st August

a drop of cognac under the parasol
        the sting of the sun
retreating its rays lighting
the vine leaves turning them
into temporary
mini-abstractions


## Perishables

Pushing through      escaping locators
& signposts like revisiting
vacated rooms
such emptiness beyond
lights in the bay a fear of gravity
ships turn on evening tide patterns of
flags raised at dusk
go your way west    to the shore
coffee house
perishables wrapped in the *Chronicle*

## The Crossing 1992
*(on the sailboat Annalise)*

You try to feed the lone bird
    blown offshore,
perched on the edge.
    You want to save it
as if trying to save your own life –
    its frayed wings, its shaking ragged coat.

The pastry chef from the five-star resort
    who craved adventure
is seasick and miserable below.
    Smoke is coming from the engine room
and a slow mysterious trickle of water
    is filling the bilge.

Outside growing seas stretch the imagination,
    humble the hunt
through every possibility or hiding place.
    Gear and paraphernalia
is thrown about the cabin.
    Then the discovery

of a broken sea cock.
    A wooden plug
banged into position brings relief.
    Later, into the night,
you sit in semi-darkness
    repairing a torn sail.
Days have gone by unaccounted for.

Now I long for the isle of Faial
    covered in blue hydrangeas
where after the crossing

we shared a late-night brandy
at the late-night café
        and felt the aura of Europe upon us.

We had turned ourselves inside out
        just to sit here, to relish
what there are no words for,
        what we barely knew ourselves –
a school of dolphins,
        the bump of a whale,

clarity and abundance.
        Land.


## Stupidly so

Luckily, and this is years ago,
the tide was coming in

when the small seagull engine
on the inflatable
wouldn't start

Determination and grit
kept me trying, stupidly so,
as I drifted

Something came over me
like I knew some over-all-being-

in-charge of fear and stupidity
on the water was watching

like I imagined
a stranger watching
or even you

standing on the wooden pier
at the bottom
of Main Street

as I was blown
from piling to piling,
when it was already too late

## In praise of a fast-moving current

that can turn as many colours as your memory
        if memory has a colour
                or even a current.

For all the times of trying to keep up with it,
        or ahead of it or knowing
                there are benefits to falling behind.

In praise of a clearer point of view,
        unknown shapes and shadows
                beneath the water –

the distance from the bottom of a rudder
        on a sailing dingy
                to the top of the waterline

before it flips on its side
        and a wave knocks it over,
                turns it around, turns you around.

How lucky you are
        not to be there
                but watching from shore,

while sand under your feet
        is pulling you down
                and the current lets you go.

# Colin Campbell Robinson

## *from* The Gap and the Flow

*A distance, a space, a gap without which, no meaning.* —Jacques Derrida

*Everything flows and nothing abides: everything gives way and nothing is fixed.*
—Heraclitus

1.

She was quickening her pace. The wind forced her on yet the rain pushed her back. She was getting nowhere. Always the gaps, the gap of space becoming time, time becoming space, she says. And the gap is me.

By chance she arrives in Paris. Visits bookshops even though her French is poor. To look at covers and feel the texture. To imbibe the perfume and visit her ancestors. The gaps must always remain open.

You will always precede me, he says.

Consider Thoth the Egyptian god of writing. What did he write?

Another gap. Are the dead present or absent? Either/or, both/and?

They sit in Le Coupole and muse over onion soup. Later, aperitifs at Le Select seeking the dead. Only grey photos remain on the walls.

~

They wandered in the rain around the industrial estate. Were her eyes silver? Were his green? Too dim to know for sure. They wondered about an inner life. Was there any place left amidst getting and spending? Would it be possible to look inside and withdraw? To cut ourselves out, she said, to create an unbridgeable gap.

The heat, the cold water bucket, the balcony at noon. She is still, the only way to be. Her religion, the view of the horizon shimmering. He, on the other hand, is closeted in an air- conditioned storehouse counting eggs. Many break and are discarded. The foreman wanders around in his grey overalls but has nothing to offer. The day will trawl the moments like every other day.

Their tears became their tears, he said recounting their story.

That night he dreamt, or experienced, he could never be sure which, a heavy being (a demon, a gargoyle, a one-eyed monster) sat on his chest making breathing difficult. No matter what pressure he exerted the being remain unmoved. Eventually, near exhaustion, he whispered her name. She heard and turned on the bedside lamp. The being vanished and he bathed in her light. Who was he? Who was she?

God cried the stars.

~

Dangerous currents swirl and we may be drawn, he said sipping his last dram. By this time she is asleep, dreaming she is asleep, dreaming. No end.

The past always present and into the future, as if this is true, she said. As if this is all a continuum and not a fragmented series of todays, tomorrows, yesterdays, billions upon billions uncounted.
Impossible mathematics.

I did not know it might be so hard to die, he said oscillating as always between speaking and thinking. Can you close the gap between truth and time? Will you wander all alone or wonder?

~

We will begin with melancholic beauty and move on from there. We will play piano and cello in the dusk and watch as the jackdaws perform their ballet of swoops and curves. Of course rain will fall intermittently and the seagulls will disrupt the concert with their material squarks.

There are traces of parts which exceed the whole he said, not the history of the dead nor the living.

La vie, la mort, she whispers.

There is only the idea of God.

## from **Contraries**

*Without contraries there is no progression.*
  —William Blake

The room is quiet not a sound all the furnishings have been removed. Listen, piano notes in the distance under whose hand?

One square, one bakery, five churches, three grocers and a bevy of doctors. There are a thousand tradesmen with violent tendencies and beautiful carers condemned to poverty. No-one else around, the street glimmers in the sun navy with a tinge of burning gold. Dogs keep a wary eye and bark at all approaches.

Behind a green door she shuffles from one chair to another seeking rest as the news invades sometimes louder, sometimes a feint buzz. Above the rooftops gulls wail as their chicks attempt flight and fail. And the Summer fair is no fun and the show reveals little so the festival is postponed.

~

Sadness can only be observed slowly.

Olive oil, lemons, the courtyard of a house and above, animated clouds breezing. Light space hear its music, liquid, heartbreaking, radiant. The weather as always languid or sharp; no matter, it is. Changing light doesn't dampen the soul only the body, damp with humidity, intoxicated by pollen: always when waking, the droplets. The door closes as light falls on the stone steps to the drying green.

~

I like being alone she says.

Paradise resides in day to day experience. A choice of roads. Follow the hill crest pine trees dark in the distance, or the river-run, white sails in the dusk, or the towpath walk, an ancient practice. Take to the South West, remember the time, furrowing fields and light. A village no one knows except those who live there, thatched and fowled in the dimming. The seekers of perfection found perfection at cost price.

Much chatter in the close the women gather with their offerings to the wind to the unseen Apollo. Dry before the patter, pitter. Their young astray in Luna light. No words to listen. These are the signs; broken petals, idle doormats, unpaired clogs. Pirate songs to wake the nearly dead to scare the spinsters as they take nightly vigil. Good news from abroad yet to be delivered. Patience. No time for prayer when there's gossip to be had to be sure.

~

Seasons weather and light, humid 22, perspiration, unusual fever and head. Not as you feel, how you remember, remember. The odours of the old town, the pleats of the beach, a stranger's bicycle balanced on the ochre wall. The wooden drawers in the wooden chest are not compliant. Such a struggle, not expected, never expected. Nothing is made by hand, chocolate and olive oil no longer created in this town. No more habits, rituals, conversation; a way of life, only a time rich with prejudices. Unable to breathe, the landscape unable to feel, the heaviness of stifling heat. In the end; no land. On another island it rains continually, never ending, never ceasing. Amen

~

Solitude with the interruption of paradox and contradiction. Nietzsche speaks of the pathos of distance, everyone to their own rhythm yet, being either neither here nor there she inhabits a zone of her own devising. Complexity is today's resistance, be difficult and walk far if they let you out. Jails are for sale on every corner, banks will give you funds so you can buy a key and snap, you're shut.

Snap; we drew the same cards.

# Ellen Harrold

## Organisation

Sometimes, I dream of taking it all off.
Layer by layer – folding
my t-shirt, my jeans, my underwear
into neat squares. My shoes on top,
socks inside. Then, I take a scissors
and cut off my hair, sweeping it into a bundle
to be set aside. My skin comes next, gently
removed and folded. Section by section.
Neat and symmetrical. Fat gathered and
laid atop. My muscles untied
from the tendons and laid in groups of two.
Each organ unravelled and gathered
like loose yarn, pulled into tight little skeins.
The nervous system – spun to a spool,
laid at the base of my brain.
Each bone clicked from cartilage and
stacked around the outskirts.
I lay it all down, in clear storage boxes
to be left in the back of the cupboard.

And I turn towards the window
to feel the breeze on my bare consciousness.
And I wake up.


## Reporting Live, from the Dissection Table

You rarely hear of a maw that's not gaping,
an abyss filled with light. Conjoined analogies,
etched into the consciousness, makes the print a bit clearer.

Sharp lines desiccated to the surface, catching on the ridges;
It bleeds out and takes a new shape. Supple and easy
against the hands, it fits without issue.

Sliding elegantly into the checklist,
no more spitting to make the ink run, clawing
at the surface, blocking the sun. Trite entitlements, hardly

enrighted to one in such a horizontal position. We can see you
in all our monitors, unravelled as the need requires.
Deviant systems purged from the records:

a wrong requires a right. Just
make sure you keep that fucker singular.
Too many and people might just start asking questions.


## Locomotion

Suck out the marrow!
The stalagnates need room
to breathe. A dance-snap
acoustic in fine-hewed din –
thunderstorm overture
set to three beats.

  1.  The clots never form. Spun to the atmosphere
with a high-octane thrum. The pounding
threads of the heartbeat match the atmosphere.

  2.  The hands reach out, cloud contortions forming
more shapes than the weather can dream. They tear
through all those chemical eruptions – set alight.

  3.  The edges always take shape. Carving new murmurations
from skylight and rainwater. Cosmic rhythms form
the orchestra – the conductor is yet to be seen.

# Aidan Semmens

## The wilds

Some things are impossibly hard to date,
feisty and flighty like the old gods,
making the world unpredictable.
Somehow the landscape has lost all meaning,

the hills hostile and all-enfolding,
evidence of the earth's indifference.
As the axis tilts back and warmer summers
melt the ice there's a hint of peat

and a beguiling herby note on the tongue.
The cliffs look traumatised, the end of land,
a place of coming and going, unsettled
like the haunting cry of the curlew.

Mycelial growth happens at the tip:
you can think of your life like this –
even as the mystery is revealed it's dismantled
and destroyed. Poets were tellers of stories,

dreamers of dreams, while all around the arena
statues of gods gazed down. I put my hand out to the fire,
felt the comforting pain like an old photograph, knowing
there would be no time to explore all we had conjured.

Now songbirds are resting in the shady trees,
yellow dogs sleeping in the sun. Clusters
of erosions can eat into the foot and hand bones;
we use the word tragic differently nowadays.

# Dancing at midnight

Lit by strobe and mirrorball,
nightclub dancers are become
devotional icons that
perfect their rituals of
martyrdom, shadows in the
dark doing the watusi
and the toxic waltz as the

camera keeps on rolling
like butchers and other gods
for now a solution to
anxieties of childhood.
TV cartoons viewed from the
safety of a shuttered room
cast a cold blue glow, every

word spoken here or there locked
up somewhere in memory;
a cruiseliner reflected
in a pale pink sea, the crew
smoking roll-ups at rusty
portholes, activists expert
in self-portraiture. What we

took for the merry dancers
is just the play of city
lights on clouds, projections of
newsreel illusion. Almost
black print on near-white sheet, all
the fictions we cannot help
but construct are a needed

way out of silence, escape
from gods and other butchers.
You know this won't end well and
perhaps it will never end

at all, for all apparent
endings are merely mirage.


## Civil Execution of Chernyshevsky

*after the painting by Nikolai Shestopalov*

By the barracks wall a man is shouting,
arm held high – in sympathy with the writer,
arch-narodnik, troublemaker-in-chief,
or revelling in the spectacle

of tsardom's pantomime justice?
In the distance the city waits,
the cathedral domes, the warehouse,
the factory and the workers

who can take no time off for the show.
Imperial ranks wait, Cossacks, dragoons,
plumed officers, infantry's green tunics.
The executioner in proud scarlet smock

awaits the order, while his prisoner,
black-robed, gazes ahead with folded hands,
listening – to the cries above the crowd,
the shuffling horses, his own thoughts?

And are we to assume he knows,
that all the military assembly knows,
what the tsar and the hangman must,
that this is all an autocratic parody,

not death itself but its public enactment,
a masquerade of martyrdom,
a mockery that might be celebration,
arms raised against raised arms?

## Bliss on Repeat

hours as a nude boy
dens were green detritus
fern and sapling
sudden scraps of porn seen
where discarded beer can ring-pulls
cut young ankle skin numb
places no light could escape from
event horizons under bracken
wide open blind spots the mystery akimbo
in the dark-thatched patch of puzzle
where her gaping legs began
our alban cocks stirred virgin

sprung leaves running
dense along the fence rails
galleried foliage screens
a ganymede cottage
by the sodden crown bowling green
gold of early barley wine
erecting sunshine in the blood
to guide the way I kid you not
find the bright and orbited body
in majesty urinal of its light
for whom the porcelain piss-stain stench
acts like catmint a cock purrs to my hand
shown the ceramic
wine-doused rim-glint
where our features float in deep cassis

a black and white snapshot
face front to camera
perched on a stack-chair
nylon-stockinged legs

crossed at the knee
back-combed hair
'68 maxi dress
anonymously pretty
suede of cork-soled sandal strap
dangled from left foot
faint in spokes of sunlight
whirring over roofs
loss it was came first thus doomed
to be mothered by bliss
long the rose burn woman gone
into hush on fire


## Molecule
*(for Valerie)*

Birdsong beyond a pattern
scratches the wind
masses and bonds
atoms and voids
makes dimension

And this would be a smooth room
walls soft hide like kid
       shadowless
    very pale
the barest hint
of blue

somewhere one can enter
anywhere they are

and find the rose burn woman gone
hush
on fire

## On open roads

On open roads, the back roads,
where they fork and markers weaken
into wood-edge then as hidden
tracks through other children's lives –
        the half-truths, leaf-trash, ivied tumble,
bits of sylvan litter teeming traps for every footfall –
from behind you origin called
and cast upon the wall you faced,
a shadow, approaching.
                            As it neared,
it shrank and densened, until completely
eclipsed by your own form.
        Then it was you turned and saw
that which all mirrors go blind to:
the subsilver, where we vanish
When reflection sleeps.


## When serene the lunar

when serene the lunar hills
shine and the unseen darken
listen to wish cut apart at sundown
the end-lulled hold on
a red-leaved lyric lost

*


moonlight is sunlight
of scant lux
        scattered
brightening nights
nights that seethe
        with stars
with silent treatment

*

stars whisper dead light down to crippled fauna
a meadows dark gradient lurches to the moon
eyes closed I see rose burn hush on fire
and from corners dawn seep a blue cause to form
ghost-white owlet wings
spans still wet with chrysalis
heaving bliss to flutter open
eyes from a dream of being borne

# John Latta

## July Notes

A barrage of thunderclaps like the sound
of sheet vinyl flooring being pulled up,
                            a dogged persistence
making the trellised clematis shake. 'Nothing new
beyond the order of the arrangement.'

*


A coppery Japanese beetle works
                its way up a mullein stalk,
dull glint in the flannel of leaves.

*


'Some fatal reticence of temperament.'

*


A field of tickseed, wild
            coreopsis, fiery yellow and red,
under a high cirrus'd sky.

Near the new pond, a spotted
            sandpiper teeters and bobs and flies
low & stiff-wingedly off.

*


Massy tangled rafts of cow vetch
intertwining and under-
                        girding
the stalks of common fleabane.

                    Form
fetches forth the relentless quotidian.

\*


To go 'beyond human ken' into
                    that querulous hive of hazard,
plausible as a goon.
                    To register
regret unperturbed by such grand insolence
as the weather delivers up
                              with its uncanny
and feckless *déménagements*.

\*


A wren in the shrubbery.

\*


Three white egrets
                    like stickpins
triangulate the debris jam-up
at the creek's elbow.

\*


Straight down rain at Mallett's Creek.
To walk is to hunch into the sluice, or sally out
against the diminuendo.
                         Useless
to look for the night heron's day haunt.

\*


Rain dashes at the gravel pit.
                         A single
Joe Pye weed blooms among pioneer grasses

& lichens.
          'Nature squanders Rigor.'

*


For we no longer love what the world's become, and so
          cop to extensions of panic, declensions of grace & lethargy,
'all this that balks delivery through words.' Close-
          companioned as patois, & articulate as grease,
we seek a form coterminous
                              with the occasion of its making.

*


A manilla folder sags with clippings,
squibs, street refuse.
                         Report of a goshawk
in the pine barrens,
                         sketch of a naked man
in blue pastel, deft vignette of a putterer.

'A careful disorderliness is the true method.'

*


(One story is that Joe Pye,
an Indian in the Massachusetts Bay Colony, concocted
of the eponymous weed a cure for typhoid fever, thus
quashing an epidemic.)

*


To perch like a kingfisher,
          a snag against the roil & froth of
          the river's unflagging composition.
To rattle off with a mechanical will.

*

A grand leaf-footed bug with orange-
                                        tipped antennae.
Clusters of midges romp in the honeysuckle.
Hart Crane: 'too jittery to write a straight sentence.'

\*


Thinking of that toothy French goof-
                                        ball Guillaume
saying, *Je ne veux pas travailler je veux fumer.*

\*


Thinking of the brashly stout
& fervently red
                    bill of the oystercatcher
ranging up & down a glacial arrangement of rocks
off Pelham Bay Park.

\*


To trigger a gloaming with a sigh, or
to register something haunting in the unintended
                                                    breakage
of the cumbrous blue, the sudden color of thinking.

\*


Out of morning's
                    unassuming ballyhoo, the *jeer*
of a jay slashes the day.

\*


A giant swallowtail works the bull thistles.
A green leopard frog stopped in the grass.
                                        Basquiat:
'I cross out words to move them into the background a bit.'

\*

*Je suis le cahier appartenant à personne.*

\*

Tilt of the green heron
     angling off the deadwood snag
examining the duckweed.

\*

Thinking of the cloud-
              suffused blue
of a tiny lake high up in the Valais,
a *piercingly* cold dip,
        white wine and raclette,
        & throwing
open the wooden shutters of the Hôtel
Weisshorn to snow in July.

\*

A Caspian tern with its black
cap pulled down low,
         all fat red bill
and unspoiled white appointment.

\*

To examine light's plumb spontaneities,
     its way of coursing down out of the sky & God
'in heuen in whose inspecte is euery regall se.'

\*

To adhere to the mad
     dazzle of ordinary things:
     adz and shaft, furrow and hoe.
To hew to the line.

\*

Thinking of *effetto di nebbia,*
        and the long song of days now gone. Dickinson:
'Life is death we're lengthy at.'

\*


To tick off the unstinting smear of ephemera—
        high white pleats of cirrocumulus, fine rain abrading
        the black belfry, blue cornflowers in a ditch—
'eye in a fine frenzy rowling.'

\*


Thinking of 'the unpedimented lions' and the casual
        way a rumpled man pinches a green paperback between thumb
and fingers.
                He is in a painting and he is skeptical
about something he is reading, lips slightly pursed, jaw slightly tensed.

\*


Cattail, yellowthroat, arrowhead, moorhen:
        to achieve a fine plenitude without
impiety or superfluousness, each thing
                'not plucked for naught.'

\*


Floody gully and dry gulch.
                        Whatever *is*
needs no justifying, the world's gone bone-
dry for love,
                and where the gods wound up
no one knows.

## A Forest Ajar Is Adjacent Glade [extract]

> Green, sheltered theatre
> or meeting place, glade.
> —Phoebe Power

Entire forest ashore on partials of glade,
foreshortened waves,
lightly chewed coasts

> Forest depths lap against this primary
> cleft, of no other torn skirting bereft

The glade itself harbours a wood's givings-out in mastly alliance, compliant
slippage, quickened residues of edge not to pierce tallness adroitly but share
a recovered breadth of light across unportable slithers    the glade is sleek of
root at just being where it is, footings resident enough

Pathos and penalties of a forest's non-extraction but porous to ground-
level interval    the scoured arena recovering a motley interlude is glade-
offer of the many totals of its alongside provision

These glade-asides (fresh assiduities)
are furtive tree-besides, the wood's
self-sown purchase of the open
not yet pervasive incursion

> the glade has its own shorn season,
> an active deferral of density,
> horizontal greens furnishing
> clearing astretch

Unabrasive inclusion at low-pressure
seclusion with no lesioning of what a forest is,
wet gashes are damping down
an opened relief of wound

A glade is both antecedent and assistive (a present eddy) defusing the harms
of vertical swarm but inbreathing the looming tree-crest which can now
be at rest, assume its own grassy alongsides are no longer an oppositional
shaded but a neutral (coated) rareness of unoccupied seething soil

Forest horizon laid on its side through which the glade transpires, hugging
a soil's stripped intimation as itself the forest's own barely given, unmasking
too many cramped multiples of ascent with this new interzone's unmasting,
delaying but still relaying the essential coasting of neighbouring pinnacles

As continue the rides and woodland
margins, insects silhouette in clear light
the allure of juxtaposed overlap, unaffronted
(freshly refaced) by uneven leapt
grades of tree density

Glade is one plant degree above
zero encumbrance, transitory episodes of
devil's bit and bugle intercede with
discrete parcels of contrary indwelling

Freshly flayed soil (clearance unseals)
instantly colonised by reserves sprouting
active seed residue, foxglove, mullein,
a patience of serving over two springs
until the small flower-cranes arise

Let them stand proud of floor, feathery mosses imitating fern, a patina
of opportunist (essential) definition, a mind of proliferating interlude

accompanies (jolts) ultimate supplanting. Given any vertical climax will always gulp at encapsulation, glade asides stay *openly* stunted by this strange miniature resumption of forest crest, too shallow for root and so shade-proof. From stolid fir to abstemious glade-stir

A woodland's shrouded meadow,
sharp strokes of bluebell pierce the pallid
ultimates of mature woodland, the canopy
is timed to its own exemptions
hollowing from within it

A glade looser than breach is ancillary forest breath, woodland's most intimate reach into and about/out of its own    basic shelter belts suspended at the onset of naked support, integral suppleness of belonging between

> Glad stony inreach, its unbarren
> barenesses yet another adept consolidation,
> scarred surfaces sustain an intermedial
> minimal green grit

Not a wrench of forest but singular splicings
of compromised declension, a new rehearsal
(no reprisal) of lack of forest at its heart

> Effective waste-weather interface

Anemones risk an eye of light into
woodland, sift fuller support
off frailty of tree

> Hesitant ground mantles, indicators
> of woodland past or imminent,
> abruptions and continuities

71

These currents of ground shuffle off pure climax forest, tree repletion can't but fan out towards local assent, new impacts of depletion, semi-prolific (with its new poverty) of engagement between. Dispersion of woodland arrayed in discrete arena, adjacency settles into a version of nearly (nearby) fulfilled accompaniment

Heavy unstable woodland become
glade-readier, resumes the open crescent of sky,
a glade its deepest interleaving

Even across the glade-flats forage a
mantled verge, swathe of huddled canopy
at insect level, dog's mercury or
green-flowered (forest-coded) spurge

Original suites of pre-forest habitat recovering their former grid across subsidence of woodland pillage, along grassy rides residual seed probes access routes    adjacency spells reversion to superseded flowers repopulating their inroads according to slightened prolifics    the paradox of oblique counter-improvement, ancient proof of lesser ways sufficing, excelling

This low-tide creep only competes with forests along its own close-woven anti-surge, opportune damage which trees can't repeat themselves with, reparation by unalike frequency

What is suddenly undisturbed in a woodland glade? This teasing apart (stripping into) a forest is the jerk/jack of distinct district modes of border suffusion, infusions of tidal grass soak into shoulder-sides unique to trees

A sliver of wood disturbance until
gladed with its non-turbulence

Glade-runners repace the splitting,
no longer a spillage of repose but
spools of repair


How does a glade guide?    Only by insinuating its vicinity, the glide
of grass will stave off containment with an interior of its own quaking,
grading its core quota of interim openness


As the vegetation dome reloops in
slender clearing     least steep flaunt of a
plant world, darts of parting without leaving


Glade supplements the scarcity
of a forest to itself

# Iain MacLeod

## Jackdaws

*for Jelle Cauwenberghs*

Like a pavilion, the spinney soft lands
In the field's near corner, moth brown and bare
This winter. Another hard winter.

Violets gather in the beaktossed mosses
For a kinder season. The copse fieldfares
Tap over the heave where wood pigeons are,

And the birch play dead in the next coppice.
Jackdaws take off like a hundred black hares
Scattergunned on through as they skim the furrs,

But assemble back in the same black hole
All aclatter. This spring they will nest here,
In a beam gap of the roofless old barn,

Dammed up against their rain, five skyblew eggs.
The fable bird waits like a shopsign there,
Pendant as a hunger artist—centre

Will that a stunned panther circles round.
Becomes the poem. Into gray open
The shells fall at thirty two feet per

       Second persecond
Out of the cloud void and up into air
Mass abounding like leaves on a zephyr—

But the sun lows, and the jackdaws settle
Down in its dipping gold. Another year
Turns up, sings the birch from grey to silver.

Just as birds, trees, we patrons of language
Root in the numb soil. But still, sometimes
I feel that we might find Byzantium.

## The Stretcher Fence

The quarry pumped all holiday. Its slate shone
Glacial black in the windows of our caravan,

And slippy as the tref railings I clung along.
A missing fleur-de-lis stump dug its rusty prong

Deep in my breast as I stretched and snatched air,
Lanced on the absence of its steel lilyflower.

Forty years before, there would have been no fence,
Just a low wall with inlaid metal nubs,

And galleries blanketed up in slatemine shafts
To keep the collection safe from the Luftwaffe.

The fences were stretchers, a municipal glean—
Easy to make, easy cleaned.

We either bury or carry our dead
In a chamber of the heart or head.

Now the stretchers are fences, round Deptford and Peckham,
Brixton—no mud on them, no wounds. Over time

They too will rust and fall, end up lost to history.
At best hope a museum piece. The quarries

Rest, roofless and washed out, their skank lakes longing
To reflect something of a shown divine.

# Iago's Orchids

Soft you, a word before you go. Salt
tears fall and soften the stones, as orchids
soften stones on the heath, or moor by and by
to chronicle the small beer, the all malt
of you, Orchid, of which every place has its native—
early marsh and purple, common, northern,
bee, green winged, frog and bog and butterfly,
the creeping tress, bird's nest, a pyramidal's
spike of perse in nebula to coral
root, southern and small white helleborine,
the twayblade—all the flowers of the field
arrayed in this, their soft phrase of peace
never speaking, before praythee the deed.
And so, a word, softly, as with your kiss.

# Luca and the Butterfly Tree
*for Elliet*

Near home there's a laburnum
that in rain hangs so heavy low
young ones shriek when they yank at it
and are covered in its yellow
clover like some lemon snowstorm.

North, on the youth hostel wall,
admirals and peacocks splay
against its magnolia stucco
whilst we sip at our plunged coffee,
both getting warmth into our souls.

The tree above us is alive
with butterflies, one alighting
on the big man's back as we slow
into day, unlike the children,
who don't know that it's life they love.

Luca pulls then lets go
a champagne panicle, as if
the chain of an old standard lamp—
but unlike the laburnum, off
they fly, up like handbird shadows

puppeted on walls. Luca stops,
and for a moment just joy
of us stirring up nature bursts
like sun on our face. And boy
does that shouldered grace drop

when the heavens open, nodding
the buddleia's globe lanterns,
splashing my coffee like stones thrown down a well.
Like monks, the butterflies fold up their wings
to one wing, one hand clapping.

# Alexander Gaul

## "Midnight. But then, a message from her arrives…"

Midnight. But then, a message from her arrives
Summoning me *now* to the place where,
She writes, "two perfect white towers
Reach into the sky and where the sweep
Of the valley between two verdant hills
Captures a secret pool where you can sip
Warm, ambrosial water, then sleep
With your cheek against the damp moss."
She does not have an innocent's gentle touch;
Desire for her is a hand clenched on the throat.

"Love will protect you on the dangerous road,"
She writes. And, certainly, the road's unlit
And demons squeal and hiss from the roadside woods
And circle the lonely traveller. Robbers
Too fall into step behind, unseen,
Until a white hand reaches from out of the dark
And plucks at the traveller's cloak. That is the test.
"Where a love's pure," she writes, "Amor will cramp
The hand of the highway thief and you will pass
Unhindered—if your love for me is true!"

"If not," she writes, and underlines the words,
"Moonbeams then will mark the road to death,
False lover, who would play me for a fool."
"What of it!" I write back. "If murdered, then
You would have to weep over my bones,
Your best dress torn, your hair loose and down,
Your perfume soured, my grave in some lonely place
Where your dramatics would go disregarded.
Consider your demands if forced to mourn!
But leave the light in your window lit. I come."

*Prop. 3.16*

78

## Two Cures for Love

[i]
Does it not live in you like a disease?

You feel the horse tremble between your knees
And test the bit and ready to let loose—
Then is the time to pull him up and not
When he's full gallop, his surging wildness stirred.

Stop at the first threshold while you can.
Starve it out when the first symptoms bite.

For, given time, the vines will groan with weight
Of tender grapes, the barren field will bloom.
The tree whose shadow shelters passers-by
Was a mean slip when planted, could have been pulled
With ease—now it dominates the square.

Try to comprehend her, and it; your neck
Withdraw from the tightening noose she puts on you.

You scoop up water from a mountain stream
That feeds the mighty Tiber: block it off
With a small rock and there is no grand river.

Myrrha watches the world from behind bark,
Transformed into a tree: stepwise one sin
Led into the next and she was doomed;
She has forever to think, "I might have stopped."

Because we love to love, get drunk on all
That Venus offers us—which is ourselves:
The girl admires you, and then you fall
For the splendid man she seems to think you are—
We postpone what must be done, and so
We cultivate those secret flames. The tree
Has roots that wrap around the heart and choke
You from within, and then you cannot hold.

[ii]
Let the fire burn out.
                    Philoctetes
Was healed after many years and struck
The winning blow in Troy. Sometimes
Delay is better than a hasty cure.

When passion's strong, give in. Who tries to swim
Against the stream when the current's strong?
Who would try to stop a mother's tears
At the graveside of her only son?

Deny the fire: you will find that it still burns!
Patience. Let the illness take its course.

*Ov. Rem Am. 79-134*

## "She was sleeping, as exhausted Ariadne…"

She was sleeping, as exhausted Ariadne
        Slept in the sand, her lover's boat retreating;
As Andromeda slept, freed at last from the rock;
        As one of the Edoni slept, her limbs
Weary from dancing, sunk in the soft grass
        Along the banks of the River Apidanus.
Her soft palm cradled her much-kissed cheek. The blanket fell
        And I could see the rise and fall of her breasts.

The torch sputtered and spat. The price of a night out
        Was coming upon her now while she was asleep—
And the reward: I missed our going to bed but then
        To see there such vulnerability—
Yes, I wanted to slide my arm under her
        And take her to me, and yet I was restrained
And gazed in wonder as Argus did at Io, changed
        By marvels so she might be better watched.

Gently I laid the garland from my head on hers,
      Tidied her tumbling hair, placed in her palm
A golden apple, though in her sleep it rolled away
      Under the blanket where I dared not reach.
She stirred and sighed and turned, and seemed to say a name.
      "What horrors stalk you in the world of dreams?"
I whispered. "Perhaps another man tries by force
      To make you his, and you call to me for help?"

The moon could have sailed past but chose instead to send
      A silver beam through the shutter slats
And her eyes flickered and opened, she caught me watching her,
      And pushed herself up on one elbow.
"You are here at last," she said, "but it's too late for love:
      Look how the stars hard as diamonds shine
And the moonlight's severe, and you come with a crown
      And a whisper. I will not be postponed!

I wove that cloth of purple there waiting for you.
      I wrote songs, sang them to myself,
Worried that you were somewhere in another's arms,
      That you were warming someone else's bed,
And that suspicion and my longing… O, my dear,
      That you had seen me weep in our room here
Until, grateful, sleep brushed me lightly with his wing,
      Your traitor's face my last imagining."

*Prop. 1.3*

## Cynthia First and Last

Rome,
      you encourage indolence
And then charge me with neglect! She's gone,
As far from me now as the River Don
Is from your shimmering streets. How, tensed
With anticipation, I felt her against
Me, heard her call me her only one,
                    Rome!
I used to please her. But the gods resent
Pleasure and men hate loyalty. Poison
Thickens with desire. Has she forgotten?
Were those kisses of no consequence,
                    Rome?


Cynthia,
      I am not steadfast;
I am not the man I was. The long
Distance from you changes me. The song
You wrote and gently sang for me is just
The memory of you singing. I am cursed
I fear, but I wish I could belong,
                    Cynthia,
To you in that moment again. I weep; the past
I bless with tears—and why prolong
Imprisonment, however sweet and wrong.
You were my first, you will be my last,
                    Cynthia.

*Prop. 1.12*

## 5

Nanti time like the present. Come on, let's get it on.
Antique omis, let 'em cackle, give us dirty looks, tut tut –
I could not give a monkey's, no, not a single fuck.
Suns can set and rise again, like brand bloody new,
but once our number's up, we're dead, that's it:
una long dark nochy for us, an endless bloody kip.
So give me una kiss, then dooey, tray.
Keep 'em coming: quarter, then chinker, then say.
Carry on: setter, then otter, then nobber…
Who's counting, got our number, keeping score?
Fuck off, you peeping tom – don't spy on our lamor.

*Nanti – no; antique – old; omi – man; cackle – talk, gossip; una – one; nochy – night; dooey- two; tray – three; quarter – four; chinker – five; say – six; setter – seven; otter – eight; nobber – nine; got your number – know that you're gay; lamor – a kiss.*

## 16

*When you assume, you make an ass out of you*

I'll charver you up the aris, stab your oyster,
you pair of pillow biters, nellies, screaming queens,
Rob, always gagging for it, total oral fixation,
and that infamous bottom, Miss Seamus O'Reilly.
Just cos my softer side comes out in my little ditties,
you goes and casts aspersions on my manhood.
Now, your artiste, he must be pure of heart,
pure in thought and deed, but not in word;
indeed, his ditties orter be a bit on the bold side,
have a wee touch of spice. It makes 'em nice.

Besides, them's the sort of ditty what gets a rise,
not out of boys, but from your antique codgers,
sad old, grey, bald heads who can no longer get it up.
You hear all about my lamors in my little ditties,
you think that means I'm growing titties?
I'll charver you up the aris, stab your oyster.

*Charver – to fuck; aris – arse; oyster – mouth; nelly – effeminate gay man; queen –*
*gay man, often effeminate; antique – old; lamor – kiss.*

## 99

My own boy chick, my darling filiome,
while you was otherwise occupied,
I half-inched a kiss – kissette, more like –
dallier than your dalliest fancy wine.
But I paid the price and then some.
Christ! You was so cross with me,
an hour or more you gave me hell.
Your Honour, I stood before the bench,
begged, wept, then wept some more;
but angry, you didn't give an inch.
Soon as I kissed you, you grabs a rag,
wipes your lips nice and clean,
nanti trace of my mooey on yours,
like you'd been pissed on by some whore.
You calls a black maria, sends for lily law;
I gets roughed up pretty good.
That dally kiss so fine as finest wine
now tasted so sour, made me sick.
If that's the price for taking without consent,
I'll go straight in future: Your Honour, I repent.

*Chicken – underage sexual partner; filiome – young man; -ette – (suffix used to turn a*
*word into Polari); dally – fine, fancy; nanti – no; mooey – mouth; lily law – the police.*

These versions use Polari, a secret language used by gay men, which flourished in London in the first seventy years or so of the twentieth century. It drew on Cockney rhyming slang as well as Parlyaree, spoken primarily by theatrical types, prostitutes, tramps, and criminals.

Polari and its milieu have a lot in common with the personal poetry of Catullus. A native of Verona in Cisalpine Gaul (that is, cis-, *on this side of* the Alps, from a Roman perspective, as opposed to trans-, *on the other side of*), Catullus was a newcomer to the city of Rome, and a young man on the make in the dying days of the Roman republic. His colourful verses welcome his readers into a world of vivid anecdotes about life and love in the city, and obscene but funny insults, often heaped up so wildly that it can be hard to take them entirely seriously. His linguistically playful poems introduce us to a cast of characters ranging from some of the most famous politicians of the day to thieves, pimps, and prostitutes. We meet Catullus' friends, his lovers, and his rivals, and as his readers we feel ourselves invited into the circle of his intimates, eavesdroppers on their everyday lives. Catullus' self-consciously subversive poems deliberately flout the standards of the stuffy older generation; he writes love poems addressed to both women and boys and he willingly adopts towards these "inferiors" what looks to Roman eyes like a pose of degrading submissiveness. He wavers between aggressive, competitive displays of his masculinity and moments of vulnerability and tenderness. His poems can be funny, sad, vicious, obscene, self-pitying, touching, sexy, colloquial, and self-consciously "literary" – sometimes within the space of a single poem.

These versions are designed to be read aloud, with a slight Cockney accent – and a great deal of camp.

# Dmitry Blizniuk

*translated by Yana Kane*

## the Lord was working out on the school blackboard

the Lord was working out, on the school blackboard
of the blue-veined starry sky,
formulas of life and death, death and death and death.
searching for proof of love,
getting so carried away He couldn't hear the sobbing and the explosions.
the children set up a slaughterhouse,
they smeared themselves with war, as if with turds and blood.
behind His back, cities became ruins,
millions of people and of lilies were annihilated.
when He was done scritching with the chalk
the last symbol on the blackboard beyond the moon,
and glanced behind Him, radiant with cold joy,
sated with perfection,
he saw the classroom—empty, destroyed by a Russian bomb,
the rubble of a Ukrainian school, roofless like the Coliseum.
shattered desks, mummified lion cubs.
and no children, no children.

## days of week went extinct like dinosaurs

days of week went extinct like dinosaurs
gone you discover
a gray bone a tusk
or the huge oar of a rib
of sunday scratchisaurus
war incinerates time warps it
ties death knots
of missile alarms
life in prison

but inside out
and everyone has been sentenced
the girl on a scooter
the soldier with a prosthetic arm
the woman walking her rottweiler


## how fantastic it is to just be

how fantastic it is to just be,
to feel alive…
your mind clear and untroubled,
like the sky before pterodactyls,
starlings, boeings, or messerschmitts,
and you—a twig that landed on a spiderweb—
you stretch out on telephone wires, not a care in the world,
like floating on your back:
not jerking, not twitching.
you're a millionaire of meaning.
and the sun shines, and the grass grows, and the spider
who hung these sunshine webs everywhere
doesn't come running for a false alarm:
he has been gobbled up by other spiders,
back before the Birth of Christ.
how awesome it is to just be and to not bother
your head with Hamlet's question.
to glance into the eyes of lovely strangers,
to shoot brazen smiley darts with confidence.
of course, to be. with you,
without you.

how fantastic
to chew on a young leaf of a plum-tree,
to look at the chestnuts in bloom—
these monstrous candelabra
with their cream-colored triangular candles.
the announcements on telephone poles, fluttering in a breeze,
flapping their telephone numbers—

like conjoined kids on swings,
dangling little legs
over a cement canyon.
a mobile phone call passes through this head of mine
a knitting needle through a jellyfish.
yet I pass through—unscathed.
in a summer café, four chairs
huddled together at a table,
like erudites from the who-where-when game show,
or mediums summoning the spirit of coca-cola.

I shake question marks from my brain,
as if tossing out pocket junk.
I don't care—I exist, that's all
I've grabbed onto the Word as if it were a dolphin;
shipwrecked,
I hurtle through the waves,
slip off.

how awesome to just be. to stride along the pavement,
to scratch the tracing paper of time with your eyes
and to leave tracks on that paper
over the tracks of others.

the simple joy of being: here's a banana,
a custard pastry,
and looking forward, attentive—
for just half a minute. sufficient for me
to preserve myself.
it's the way a chess player sweeps the pieces off the board
and looks at the face reflected in the varnish:
the fiery crab of a chandelier;
that's how to reboot yourself.
there are a few minutes to be distracted,
to turn your attention to the world:
on the scales everything is in perfect balance—inside and out,
the hummingbird feather and the kettlebell.
everyone has this feeling:

an empty airport in the early morning,
and an old man, the skin on his neck sagging like a Komodo dragon,
strolling along the cool concrete.


## the embassy of dreams

they used to pick up sleds, and their friends,
and the bunch of them—jubilant, huffing—
would go to the pine hill to sled
right under the noses of cathedral spire pines;
frost captured the air in clusters of icy piranhas,
and every inhale-exhale had to be torn off
space, like stickers off backpacks. are you picturing this?
and a girl, with her ruddy peach cheeks, was there,
and the blue-white-gold city looked
with lazy indifference
at the small, lively scrap of childhood in the very centre—
the way a robot looks, without comprehension,
at a living human sprout,
or a poem by a high school freshman.
childhood is a magic circle chalked around Gogol.
it scares off all the revolting, calculating ghouls,
wards off the flamboyant monsters
of adult life.
alas, the fairy-tale armour wears thin,
and behind the brand-new high-rises hides a vacant lot
and its corpses of cats and dogs, and its lairs of drifters.
but right now, he looks at the girl, and he sees a snow crystal.
the snow crystal whoops, laughs, and brushes back her bangs,
wet with melted snow and fresh sweat.
who knows what kind of ice queen
or big-breasted snow effigy she'll become with time.
some among them destined to be a drug addict,
a thief, a drunkard, or a common floozy.
but now they are under the protection of childhood.
the embassy of dreams—with its rosy windows
and parrot Kesha from old cartoons,

with the adorably cocooned cussing—
is keeping them safe for the time being.
and as he grows, he will walk time after time over the pine hill
with his girlfriend and a beer, and later, with big-eyed silence,
listening deeply to the vibrating violoncello of the pine trees and the sky,
taking in the gossip of scraggly squirrels,
and only dimly aware that he is crossing the promised land,
the lost earthly paradise that flashed by like a snapshot,
like a life, like a rainstorm from the translucent fingers
of a virtuoso pianist; and the horizontal rainstorm of days
flows together into spidery, crab-like, swift radiance…

NOTE
The first two poems above were written during wartime; the final two are pre-war poems.

The translator is grateful to Bruce Esrig for editing the final texts.

# Vicente Huidobro

*translated by Tony Frazer*

## *from* Altazor ( Canto III — beginning )

Woman the world is furnished by your eyes
The sky rises higher in your presence
The earth extends from rose to rose
And the air extends from dove to dove

When you depart you leave a star in your place
You lower your lights like a passing boat
While my enchanted song follows you
Like a faithful and melancholy snake
And you turn your head around behind some star

What battle is being fought in space?
Those spears of light between planets
Reflected off merciless armour
What bloodthirsty star refuses to step aside?
Where are you sad night-walker
Giver of infinity
Wandering through the forest of dreams

Here I am lost amongst desolate seas
Alone like a feather falling from a bird at night
Here I am in a tower of cold
Wrapped in the memory of your oceanic lips
In the memory of your pleasure and of your hair
Shining and loose like mountain rivers
Would you be blind if God had not given you such hands?
I ask you again

The arch of your brow drawn for the weapons of your eyes
In the victorious winged offensive secure with pride in its flowers
The modest stones speak to you for me

The waves of birds with no sky speak to you for me
The colour of windless landscapes speaks to you for me
The flock of sullen sheep speaks to you for me
Asleep in your memory
The revealed stream speaks to you for me
The surviving herbs tied to the adventure
Adventure of light and blood on the horizon
With no shelter but a flower that is snuffed out
Whenever there is a little wind

The plains are lost under your fragile grace
The world is lost beneath your visible passage
For everything is artifice when you appear
With your dangerous light
Innocent harmony with no fatigue or forgetfulness
Something like tears rolling inwards
Built out of haughty fear and silence

You make time doubt
And the sky too with its instinct for infinity
Far from you everything is mortal
You strew agony across a humiliated land of night
Only those that think of you can taste eternity

Here is your star passing by
With your breathing wearied by distance
With your gestures and the way you walk
With the magnetised space greeting you
Putting leagues of night between us

Yet I warn you we are stitched
To the same star
We are stitched by the same music stretched
From one to the other
By the same giant shadow shaking like a tree
Let us be that piece of sky
That fragment where the mysterious adventure takes place
The adventure of the planet that bursts into dream petals

In vain would you try to evade my voice
And vault the walls of my praise
We are stitched by the same star
You are tethered to the moon nightingale
That carries a sacred ritual in its throat
What do I care for the signs of night
And the roots and funereal echoes they make in my chest
What do I care for the shining enigma
The symbols shining a light upon chance
And those islands that wander aimlessly through chaos to my eyes
What do I care for that flower's fear in the void
What do I care for the name of nothingness
The name of the infinite desert
Or of the will or chance they represent
And if in that desert each star is a yearning for an oasis
Or banners of premonition and death

I have an atmosphere of my own in your breath
The fabulous confidence of your gaze with its intimate constellations
With its own seed-like language
Your brow shining like one of God's rings
Firmer than all the flora in the sky
Without the whirlwinds of the universe rearing up
Like a horse seeing its own shadow in the air

I ask you again
Were you meant to be mute that God gave you such eyes?

That voice of yours is all the defence I need
That voice which emerges from you in heartbeats
That voice where eternity falls
And shatters into fragments of phosphorescent orbs

What would life be like if you had never been born?
A comet with no mantle dying of cold

[ ... ]

# César Vallejo

*translated by Valentino Gianuzzi*

## Christmas

Drowning in the incessant racket of Chaldean idiots and belated Tyrians, with my imperial silence I let the evening pass, assisted by fierce, unbeatable dreams, as I call on the pain—tolling bell, tolling bell, tolling bell!

Today snowy Noel, a distant Hebrew, with his amazing grandfatherly hands, will set by the poor children's bedsides a wonderful toy or a sweet chocolate, a present from Baby Jesus to his friends down here.

Today will be Christmas; and it will arrive so sadly, so mournfully, in my eyes of Yuletide, in my eyes of a shepherd lonely and lost.

And so you will bleat on, sheep of mine, sheep of the lord, sweet droplets of breastmilk from the Virgin Mary.

# A Note on 'Christmas'

In 2024, a previously unknown poem by César Vallejo was rediscovered in the Peruvian press by Wilmer Cutipa Luque. The poem had been originally published in the Lima daily *La Prensa*, on 25 December 1918, and had remained in the oblivion of the archive for more than a century. Quite inexplicably, Vallejo did not include this composition, titled 'Navidad', in his first book of poems, *The Black Heralds*, which would be published six months later. It would surely not be out of place in that book, due to its use of Biblical imagery. What sets it apart from other compositions in *The Black Heralds*, however, is that it is a prose poem. Perhaps Vallejo wanted to save it and include it in his second book, *Trilce*, but the later adoption of avant-garde aesthetics made 'Navidad' increasingly less fitting among *Trilce*'s more radical poetics. Dedicated to his father, the poem must have been close to Vallejo's heart, but aesthetic rigour demanded a kill-your-darlings approach.

In any case, 'Navidad' is still an important composition in Vallejo's *oeuvre*. More evidently, the poem is inspired by the death of his mother (in August 1918), who presides over the speaker's mournful tone and makes a metonymic appearance as the universal mother: the Virgin Mary. Less evidently, 'Navidad' is an *ars poetica* which associates suffering and sadness with inspiration, and which contrasts the overly intellectual (Chaldean idiots – perhaps a reference to the Wise Men) and outdated writers (belated Tyrians) with the more down-to-earth actions of the suffering shepherd poet, true prophet of a new beginning.

This is the first translation of the poem.

Valentino Gianuzzi

# Notes on Contributors

**OPHIRA ADAR** is a poet and writer from London, whose work has appeared in *Poetry Wales, Under The Radar, Butcher's Dog, 14 magazine* and *Full House Literary*. Her pamphlet *Say I Am Not Your Mother* was highly commended in the 2025 International Book and Pamphlet Competition by The Poetry Business. She holds an MA (distinction) in Writing Poetry from The Poetry School.

**ALAN BAKER** was born and raised in Newcastle-upon-Tyne and has lived in Nottingham since 1985 where runs the poetry publisher Leafe Press. His recent books include *Riverrun*, a series of modernist sonnets about the river Trent, and *Early One Morning*, a collaboration with the artist Rebecca Forster. Shearsman Books will publish *A Book of Psalms* in 2026.

**DMITRY BLIZNIUK** is a poet from Kharkiv, Ukraine. He has authored several collections of poetry in Russian. *The Red Forest*, a book of his poetry translated into English, was published by Fowlpox Press (Canada) in 2018. *По Той Бік Попелу* (On the Other Side of the Ashes), a book of his poetry that he translated into Ukrainian, was published in Ukraine by Herda in 2024.

**GAIUS VALERIUS CATULLUS** (c.84 BC—c.54 BC) was a poet of Ancient Rome, born to a patrician family in Verona. Some 114 of his poems survive.

**IAN DAVIDSON**'s most recent poetry publications are *Just a Line to Let you Know* (Crater 2024), *The Matter of the Heart* (Red Squirrel 2023) and *By Tiny Twisting Ways* (Aquifer 2021). His critical and scholarly writing has been published in monographs, journal articles and essays. A new poetry collection *And Why Not* is in preparation for publication in 2026, and he has just completed a new critical book called *Out of Place*. Originally from Cymru/Wales, he is Professor of Poetry in University College Dublin and lives and works on a small farm in County Mayo, Ireland.

**ADAM FLINT** was born in North London and is currently based in Berlin. Previous poems have appeared in *Blackbox Manifold, Poetry Salzburg Review, Shearsman* magazine, *Stand* and *The Rialto*, among others.

**TONY FRAZER** is publisher of Shearsman Books and founding editor of this magazine. He is engaged in a long-running project to bring the entire mature output of Huidobro into English, including poetry, essays and fiction. (Dramatic works and polemics are being left out, at least for now.)

**ALEXANDER GAUL** lives in Ireland. The work in this issue is a small selection of "Roman" poems from a book-length sequence of versions or poems "after" a number of poets including Propertius, Catullus, Horace, Virgil, Tibullus, Ovid, and others. The sequence is called *The End of the Affair*.

**VALENTINO GIANUZZI** is a Peruvian scholar teaching at the University of Manchester. He edited and co-translated all of the Vallejo volumes published by Shearsman Books.

**JOHN GOODBY** is the author of several books on Dylan Thomas, among them *Under the Spelling Wall: the Poetry of Dylan Thomas* (2013). His poetry collections include *Illennium* (Shearsman, 2010) and *The No Breath, The Ars and So, Rise* (Red Ceilings, 2017–2022). Collaborative works include *Giraldus Redivivus* (Incunabula, 2024) and *Ätherstrophen*, versionings of Emmy Hemmings (ZimZalla, 2025), with David Annwn, and he co-edited *The Edge of Necessary: Welsh Innovative Poetry 1966–2018* (Aquifer, 2018) with Lyndon Davies.

**LUCY HAMILTON**'s third Shearsman book *Viewer / Viewed* (2023) is a collection of her handmade photo-montages and accompanying ekphrastic poems. Prose poems from her current work-in-progress, *Reverse : Inverse,* have appeared in *The Fortnightly Review, Tears in the Fence, Shearsman* magazine, *Dreaming Awake: New Contemporary Prose Poetry from the United States, Australia, and the United Kingdom* (Madhat Press, Vermont, 2023), *Blackbox Manifold,* and are forthcoming in *Campella Poetry Journal.*

**ELLEN HARROLD** is an Irish artist, writer and editor-in-chief of *Metachrosis Literary.* She uses painting, drawing, text, and textiles to explore anatomy and physics through creative abstraction. She has exhibited her art with the Irish Museum of Modern Art (*Earth Rising*, 2024), Lido Stores Margate (*If Heaven Falls*, 2025), and Newcastle Arts Centre (*Confluences*, 2024). She has also recently published art in *The Storms, An Áitiúil,* and *Orion.* She has published poetry in English and Irish in magazines such as *Shearsman, The Pomegranate,* and *Channel.*

**LYNNE HJELMGAARD** has published five books of poetry, the most recent being *The Turpentine Tree* (Seren Books, 2023).

**VICENTE HUIDOBRO** (1893–1948) was a leading figure in the first phase of the Hispanic and Latin American avant-garde, bringing into Spanish lessons learned from French poets such as Apollinaire, Reverdy and Jacob. His work settled down in the mid-1920s into a recognisable style that stayed with him until the end, 2 decades later, its rhetoric heavily influenced by Surrealism. *Altazor* (1931) is a book-length poem widely considered to be his masterpiece, but one which has taken quite some time to attain the status it now possesses. The complete translation will appear from Shearsman Books in 2026.

**JENNIFER INGLEHEART** is Professor of Latin at Durham University and has published widely on Latin poetry and its reception (including Catullus). She was curator of an exhibition of banned books (*Story of Phi*) at the Bodleian Library and has performed her work at Polari Literary Salon. Her long-standing interests in queer translation and LGBTQ history have led her to write versions of Catullus in Polari.

**YANA KANE** came to the United States as a refugee from the Soviet Union. She holds a BSE degree in Electrical Engineering and Computer Science from Princeton University, a PhD in Statistics from Cornell University, and an MFA in Creative Writing with a concentration in Literary Translation from Fairleigh Dickinson University. She won the 2024 RHINO Poetry Translation Prize, was a finalist for the 2024 Gabo Prize for Literature in Translation, was selected for the 2025 Deep Vellum Best Literary Translations Anthology, and has been nominated for the 2026 Deep Vellum *Best Literary Translations Anthology*. Since early 2022, over 30 of her original English-language poems, short stories, and essays, as well as over 30 of her translations of poetry have appeared or are forthcoming in literary magazines in the UK and the USA. Her translations and original poetry both appeared in *Dislocation* (2024, Indiana University's Slavica Press), an anthology of English translations of Russophone anti-war poetry.

**PETER LARKIN** has published many books, a large number of them with Shearsman. His most recent is *Scarcely Carry All Vast Woods* (Shearsman Books, 2025)

**JOHN LATTA**'s first collection, *Rubbing Torsos*, was published by Ithaca House in 1979. His second, *Breeze*, was published in 2003 by the University of Notre Dame Press. *Some Alphabets* was published in 2022 by Luigi Ballerini in the Opuntia Series of Agincourt Press. Recent poems in *The Brooklyn Rail, Critical Quarterly, Oversound, Hurricane Review, Notre Dame Review, Lana Turner,* and *Blackbox Manifold*. For some years (2006–2015) he blogged regularly at *Isola di Rifiuti*.

**DOROTHY LEHANE** is the author of the following poetry publications: *Eight Songs of [Mothering] & [Capacity]* (Guillemot Press), *House Girl* (Aquifer Press), *I'm Very Interested in Falling in Love With You* (Run Amok Press) *Bettbehandlung* (Muscaliet Press), *Umwelt* (Leafe Press), *Ephemeris* (Nine Arches Press) and *Places of Articulation* (dancing girl press). Until the summer of 2023, she was Senior Lecturer in Creative Writing at the University of Kent. She is currently working on a variety of outputs about caves, funded by grants from the British Academy / Leverhulme, The Society of Authors, and the Arts Council.

**IAIN MACLEOD** works as a bookseller in Glasgow, and has done so for almost 20 years. He began writing short fiction approximately 5 years ago, and has been writing poems for the last 3. One of his poems appeared in the anthology *Green Verse* (Saraband, 2024).

**COLIN CAMPBELL ROBINSON** is a writer and photographer living in Edinburgh and on the Isle of Bute. Knives Forks and Spoons Press published his books *Blue Solitude* in 2018, *Footnotes from History – the Debord Variations* in 2021 and *Resistance* in 2025.

**PETER ROBINSON**'s *Collected Poems 1976–2016* (2017), *The Personal Art: Essays, Reviews & Memoirs* (2021), and *Peter Robinson: A Portrait of his Work* (ed Tom Phillips, 2021) are published by Shearsman Books. *Return to Sendai: New & Selected Poems 1973–2024* recently appeared in the USA from MadHat Press.

**BILJANA SCOTT** was born in Switzerland to Scottish-Serbian/Croatian parents. Recent poems have appeared in the 2025 issues of *The Pomegranate* and *Wells Street Journal*, and 2024 issues of *Tears in the Fence, Long Poem Magazine, 14 Magazine, Acumen, Poetry Scotland, London Grip, Noon* and Joy Howard's anthology *Two Ravens*.

**AIDAN SEMMENS**, winner of the Scottish Poetry Library's Julia Budenz Commemorative Prize and the 2024 Mallaig Book Festival Deirdre Roberts Prize, lives in Orkney. He is the author of six poetry collections, four of which are from Shearsman Books, which will also publish his next collection, *Signals from the Disappearing Shore*, in 2026.

**PENELOPE SHUTTLE** has lived in Cornwall since 1970. Her first collection of poems, The Orchard Upstairs (1981) was followed by six other books from Oxford University Press. Her retrospective, *Unsent: New & Selected Poems 1980–2012* (Bloodaxe Books,

2012), drew on ten collections published over three decades plus the title-collection, *Unsent*. Her later collections from Bloodaxe are *Will you walk a little faster?* (2017) and the double collection *Lyonesse* (2021), which was longlisted for the Laurel Prize 2022. *Heath*, a collaboration about Hounslow Heath with John Greening, was published by Nine Arches in 2016.

**ANDREW TAYLOR** has published four collections with Shearsman Books. The latest, *European Hymns* was published in September 2024. A recent critical book, *There's Everything to Play For: The Poetry of Peter Finch* was published by Seren Books in March 2025.

**STEVEN TAYLOR** is currently working on a collection of poems called *HYDE* which is about coal mining, cotton and culture. He has had over 500 poems published in various magazines and periodicals including *Shearsman, Acumen, Magma, The North, Orbis, Stand, Urthona* and *The Wallace Stevens Journal*. His work appeared in The Poetry Business *Coal* anthology in 2024 and *Buzzin Bards* anthology in 2025.

**CÉSAR VALLEJO** (1892–1938) was the greatest Peruvian poet of the 20th century, and a figure of enormous importance in Hispanic letters. Shearsman Books have published all of his poetry, but the poem here has only recently been rediscovered. It will be included in our revised version of the poet's *Complete Poems* in 2026.

## Titles Recently Listed for Awards

Measures of Weather
J. R. Carpenter

A Cranic of Ordinaries

Eliza O'Toole

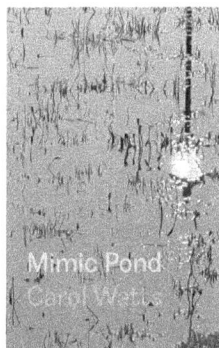

Mimic Pond
Carol Watts

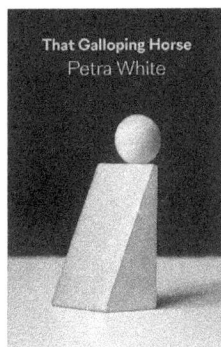

That Galloping Horse
Petra White

THE LOST BOOK OF BARKINGE

Bridget Khursheed
Exact Colour of Snow

www.ingramcontent.com/pod-product-compliance
Lightning Source LLC
Chambersburg PA
CBHW020907100426
42737CB00044B/618